TRANSLATED

Translated Language Learning

Aladdin and the Wonderful Lamp

アラジンと不思議なランプ

Antoine Galland

English / 日本語

Copyright © 2023 Tranzlaty
All rights reserved
Published by Tranzlaty
ISBN: 978-1-83566-066-9
Original text by Antoine Galland
From *"Les mille et une nuits"*
First published in French in 1704
Taken from The Blue Fairy Book
Collected and translated by Andrew Lang
www.tranzlaty.com

Aladdin and the Wonderful Lamp
アラジンと不思議なランプ

Once upon a time there lived a poor tailor
むかしむかし、貧しい仕立て屋が住んでいました
he had a son called Aladdin
彼にはアラジンという息子がいた
Aladdin was a careless, idle boy who would do nothing
アラジンは、何もしない無頓着で怠惰な少年でした
although, he did like to play ball all day long
しかし、彼は一日中ボールで遊ぶのが好きでした
this he did in the streets with other little idle boys
これは、彼が他の小さな怠惰な男の子たちと一緒に通りでやったことです
This so grieved the father that he died
これは父親をとても悲しませたので、彼は死にました
his mother cried and prayed but nothing helped
母親は泣き叫び、祈ったが、何の役にも立たなかった
despite her pleading, Aladdin did not mend his ways
彼女の懇願にもかかわらず、アラジンは彼のやり方を改めませんでした
One day Aladdin was playing in the streets as usual
ある日、アラジンはいつものように街で遊んでいました
a stranger asked him his age
見知らぬ人が彼に年齢を尋ねた
and he asked him if he was not the son of Mustapha the tailor
そして、自分は仕立て屋ムスタファの息子ではないかと尋ねた
"I am the son of Mustapha, sir" replied Aladdin
「私はムスタファの息子です」とアラジンは答えました
"but he died a long time ago"
「でも、とっくの昔に死んでしまった」
the stranger was a famous African magician

その見知らぬ男は有名なアフリカの魔術師だった
and he fell on his neck and kissed him
そして、彼の首にひれ伏し、彼に接吻した
"I am your uncle" said the magician
「私はあなたの叔父さんです」と魔術師は言いました
"I knew you from your likeness to my brother"
「お前が兄に似ていたからお前を知っていた」
"Go to your mother and tell her I am coming"
「お母さんのところに行って、私が行くと伝えてください」
Aladdin ran home and told his mother of his newly found uncle
アラジンは家に走って帰り、新しく見つけた叔父のことを母親に話しました
"Indeed, child," she said, "your father had a brother"
「ほんとうに、お嬢さん」と彼女は言った、「あなたのお父さんには兄弟がいたのよ」
"but I always thought he was dead"
「でも、私はいつも彼が死んだと思っていました」
However, she prepared supper for the visitor
しかし、彼女は訪問者のために夕食を用意しました
and she bade Aladdin to seek his uncle
そして彼女はアラジンに叔父を探すように命じました
Aladdin's uncle came laden with wine and fruit
アラジンの叔父さんがワインと果物を積んでやって来ました
He fell down and kissed the place where Mustapha used to sit
彼は倒れ込み、ムスタファが座っていた場所にキスをした
and he bid Aladdin's mother not to be surprised
そして、アラジンの母親に驚かないように言いました
he explained he had been out of the country forty years
彼は40年間国を離れていたと説明した

He then turned to Aladdin and asked him his trade
それから彼はアラジンに向き直り、彼の取引を尋ねました
but the boy hung his head in shame
しかし、少年は恥ずかしそうに頭を垂れました
and his mother burst into tears
母親は泣き出した
so Aladdin's uncle offered to provide food
そこで、アラジンの叔父さんが食べ物を提供すると申し出ました

The next day he bought Aladdin a fine suit of clothes
次の日、彼はアラジンに立派な服を買ってあげました
and he took him all over the city
そして、彼は彼を町中に連れて行きました
he showed him the sights of the city
彼は彼に街の光景を見せました
at nightfall he brought him home to his mother
日が暮れると、彼は彼を母親のところに連れて帰りました
his mother was overjoyed to see her son so fine
母親は息子が元気な姿を見て大喜びでした
The next day the magician led Aladdin into some beautiful gardens
次の日、マジシャンはアラジンを美しい庭園に連れて行きました
this was a long way outside the city gates
ここは城門から遠く離れたところにあった
They sat down by a fountain
二人は噴水のそばに腰を下ろした
and the magician pulled a cake from his girdle
そして手品師はガードルからケーキを取り出しました
he divided the cake between the two of them
彼はケーキを二人に分けました

Then they journeyed onward till they almost reached the mountains
それから二人は、ほとんど山にたどり着くまで旅を続けました
Aladdin was so tired that he begged to go back
アラジンはとても疲れていたので、帰りたいと懇願しました
but the magician beguiled him with pleasant stories
しかし、魔術師は愉快な話で彼を惑わした
and he led him on in spite of his laziness
そして、怠惰にもかかわらず、彼を導いた
At last they came to two mountains
とうとう二人は二つの山に着きました
the two mountains were divided by a narrow valley
2つの山は狭い谷で分かれていた
"We will go no farther" said the false uncle
「これ以上は行かないよ」と偽叔父は言いました
"I will show you something wonderful"
「素敵なものをお見せします」
"gather up sticks while I kindle a fire"
「火を焚きながら棒を集めて」
When the fire was lit the magician threw a powder on it
火が灯されると、魔術師は火に粉を投げました
and he said some magical words
そして、彼は魔法の言葉を言いました
The earth trembled a little and opened in front of them
大地が少し揺れて、目の前に広がった
a square flat stone revealed itself
四角い平らな石が姿を現した
and in the middle of the the stone was a brass ring
そして石の真ん中には真鍮の指輪がありました
Aladdin tried to run away
アラジンは逃げようとした
but the magician caught him

しかし、魔術師は彼を捕まえました
and gave him a blow that knocked him down
そして彼をノックダウンする打撃を与えました
"What have I done, uncle?" he said piteously
「おじさん、僕は何をしてしまったんだい?」彼は哀れみを込めて言った
the magician said more kindly: "Fear nothing, but obey me"
魔術師はもっと親切に言いました:「何も恐れることはないが、私に従いなさい」
"Beneath this stone lies a treasure which is to be yours"
「この石の下には、あなたのものになる宝物があります」
"and no one else may touch it"
「そして、他の誰もそれに触れてはならない」
"so you must do exactly as I tell you"
「だから、お前は俺の言うとおりにしろ」
At the mention of treasure Aladdin forgot his fears
宝物の話で、アラジンは恐怖を忘れました
he grasped the ring as he was told
彼は言われたとおりに指輪を握りしめた
and he said the names of his father and grandfather
そして、父と祖父の名前を言った
The stone came up quite easily
石は簡単に上がってきました
and some steps appeared in front of them
そして、彼らの前にいくつかのステップが現れました
"Go down" said the magician
「下がれ」と魔術師は言った
"at the foot of those steps you will find an open door"
「その階段の足元には、開いた扉があります」
"the door leads into three large halls"
「扉は3つの大きなホールに通じている」
"Tuck up your gown and go through the halls"
「ガウンをたくし上げて廊下を抜ける」

"make sure not to touching anything"
「何も触らないように気をつけて」
"if you touch anything, you will die instantly"
「何かに触ると即死する」
"These halls lead into a garden of fine fruit trees"
「これらのホールは、立派な果樹の庭に通じています」
"Walk on until you come to a niche in a terrace"
「テラスのくぼみに来るまで歩き続ける」
"there you will see a lighted lamp"
「そこに灯ったランプが見えます」
"Pour out the oil of the lamp"
「ランプの油を注ぐ」
"and then bring me the lamp"
「それからランプを持ってきて」
He drew a ring from his finger and gave it to Aladdin
彼は指から指輪を取り出し、アラジンに渡しました
and he bid him to prosper
そして、彼は彼に繁栄するように命じました
Aladdin found everything as the magician had said
アラジンは魔術師が言ったようにすべてを見つけました
he gathered some fruit off the trees
彼は木から果物を集めました
and, having got the lamp, he arrived at the mouth of the cave
そして、ランプを持って、洞窟の入り口に着きました
The magician cried out in a great hurry
魔術師は大慌てで叫びました
"Make haste and give me the lamp"
「急いでランプをください」
This Aladdin refused to do until he was out of the cave
このアラジンは、洞窟から出るまで拒否しました
The magician flew into a terrible passion
魔術師は恐ろしい情熱に飛び込みました
he threw some more powder on to the fire

彼は火に火をくべた
and then he cast another magic spell
そして、彼はまた魔法の呪文を唱えた
and the stone rolled back into its place
そして石は元の場所に転がり戻った
The magician left Persia for ever
魔術師は永遠にペルシャを去った
this plainly showed that he was no uncle of Aladdin's
これは、彼がアラジンの叔父ではないことをはっきりと示しました
what he really was was a cunning magician
彼の正体は狡猾な魔術師だった
a magician who had read of a wonderful lamp
素晴らしいランプを読んだ魔術師
a lamp which would make him the most powerful man in the world
彼を世界で最も強力な男にするランプ
but he alone knew where to find it
しかし、彼だけがそれを見つける場所を知っていました
and he could only receive it from the hand of another
そして、彼はそれを他の人の手からしか受け取ることができませんでした
He had picked out the foolish Aladdin for this purpose
彼はこの目的のために愚かなアラジンを選んだのです
he had intended to get the lamp and kill him afterwards
彼はランプを手に入れて、後で彼を殺すつもりでした

For two days Aladdin remained in the dark
2日間、アラジンは暗闇の中にいました
he cried and lamented his situation
彼は泣き叫び、自分の状況を嘆いた
At last he clasped his hands in prayer
とうとう彼は両手を握りしめて祈りました
and in so doing he rubbed the ring

そして、そうして指輪をこすった
the magician had forgotten to take the ring back from him
魔術師は指輪を取り戻すのを忘れていた
Immediately an enormous and frightful genie rose out of the earth
たちまち、巨大で恐ろしい魔神が大地から現れた
"What would thou have me do?"
「お前は俺に何をさせるつもりだ?」
"I am the Slave of the Ring"
「私は指輪の奴隷」
"and I will obey thee in all things"
「わたしはすべてのことにおいてあなたに従います」
Aladdin fearlessly replied: "Deliver me from this place!"
アラジンは大胆不敵に「私をこの場所から救い出してください!」と答えました。
and the earth opened above him
そして、大地が彼の上に開いた
and he found himself outside
そして、気がつくと彼は外にいた
As soon as his eyes could bear the light he went home
彼の目が光に耐えられるようになるとすぐに、彼は家に帰りました
but he fainted when he got there
しかし、彼はそこに着いたときに気を失いました
When he came to himself he told his mother what had happened
我に返ったとき、彼は母親に何が起こったのかを話しました
and he showed her the lamp
そして、ランプを彼女に見せました
and he shower her the the fruits he had gathered in the garden

そして、庭で集めた果物を娘に浴びせました
the fruits were, in reality, precious stones
果物は、実際には宝石でした
He then asked for some food
それから彼は食べ物を頼みました
"Alas! child" she said
「ああ！子供」と彼女は言った
"I have nothing in the house"
「家には何もない」
"but I have spun a little cotton"
「でも、少し綿を紡いでいる」
"and I will go and sell the cotton"
「綿花を売りに行こう」
Aladdin bade her keep her cotton
アラジンは彼女に綿を保つように命じた
he told her he would sell the lamp instead of the cotton
彼は彼女に、綿の代わりにランプを売ると言いました
As it was very dirty she began to rub the lamp
とても汚れていたので、ランプをこすり始めました
a clean lamp might fetch a higher price
きれいなランプはより高い値段で取引されるかもしれません
Instantly a hideous genie appeared
たちまち恐ろしい魔神が現れた
he asked what she would like to have
彼は彼女が何が欲しいか尋ねました
at the sight of the genie she fainted
魔神を見て、彼女は気を失った
but Aladdin, snatching the lamp, said boldly:
しかし、アラジンはランプをひったくり、大胆に言いました。
"Fetch me something to eat!"
「何か食べるものを持ってきて！」
The genie returned with a silver bowl

精霊は銀の鉢を持って戻ってきた
he had twelve silver plates containing rich meats
彼は豊かな肉の入った銀の皿を12枚持っていました
and he had two silver cups and two bottles of wine
そして、銀の杯を二つとぶどう酒を二本持っていました
Aladdin's mother, when she came to herself, said:
アラジンの母親は、我に返ったとき、こう言いました。
"Whence comes this splendid feast?"
「この華麗なご馳走はどこから来るの?」
"Ask not where it came from, but eat, mother" replied Aladdin
「どこから来たのかは聞かないで、食べなさい、お母さん」とアラジンは答えました
So they sat at breakfast till it was dinner-time
それで、夕食の時間まで朝食に座っていました
and Aladdin told his mother about the lamp
そしてアラジンは母親にランプのことを話しました
She begged him to sell it
彼女は彼にそれを売るように懇願した
"let us have nothing to do with devils"
「悪魔とは何の関係もない」
but Aladdin had thought it would be wiser to use the lamp
しかし、アラジンはランプを使う方が賢明だと考えていました
"chance hath made us aware of its virtues"
「偶然は、その美徳に気づかせた」
"we will use it, and the ring likewise"
「私たちはそれを使います。指輪も同様に使います」
"I shall always wear it on my finger"
「いつまでも指にはめておく」
When they had eaten all the genie had brought, Aladdin sold one of the silver plates

精霊が持ってきたものを全部食べ終えると、アラジンは銀の皿を1つ売りました

and when he needed money again he sold the next plate
そして、またお金が必要になったとき、次の皿を売りました

he did this until no plates were left
彼は皿がなくなるまでこれを続けました

He then he made another wish to the genie
それから彼は精霊に別の願い事をしました

and the genie gave him another set of plates
そして魔神は彼にもう一組の皿をくれました

and thus they lived for many years
こうして、彼らは何年も生きた

One day Aladdin heard an order from the Sultan
ある日、アラジンはスルタンからの命令を聞きました

everyone was to stay at home and close their shutters
みんな家にいて、雨戸を閉める

the Princess was going to and from her bath
お姫様はお風呂に行ったり来たりしていました

Aladdin was seized by a desire to see her face
アラジンは自分の顔を見たいという欲求にとらわれました

although it was very difficult to see her face
彼女の顔を見るのはとても難しかったですが

because everywhere she went she wore a veil
どこへ行ってもベールをかぶっていたからだ

He hid himself behind the door of the bath
彼は浴槽の扉の後ろに身を隠した

and he peeped through a chink in the door
そして、ドアの隙間から覗いた

The Princess lifted her veil as she went in to the bath
お姫様はベールを持ち上げてお風呂に入りました

and she looked so beautiful that Aladdin fell in love with her at first sight
そして、彼女はとても美しく見えたので、アラジンは彼女に一目惚れしました

He went home so changed that his mother was frightened
家に帰ると、母親が怯えるほど変わってしまいました

He told her he loved the Princess so deeply that he could not live without her
彼は王女を深く愛しているので、彼女なしでは生きていけないと彼女に言いました

and he wanted to ask her in marriage of her father
そして、彼は彼女の父親の結婚で彼女に尋ねたかったのです

His mother, on hearing this, burst out laughing
それを聞いた母親は大笑いした

but Aladdin at last prevailed upon her to go before the Sultan
しかし、アラジンはついにスルタンの前に行くように彼女を説得しました

and she was going to carry his request
そして、彼女は彼の要求を運ぶつもりでした

She fetched a napkin and laid in it the magic fruits
彼女はナプキンを取ってきて、その中に魔法の実を置きました

the magic fruits from the enchanted garden
魅惑の庭の魔法の果実

the fruits sparkled and shone like the most beautiful jewels
果物は最も美しい宝石のようにきらめき、輝いていました

She took the magic fruits with her to please the Sultan
彼女はスルタンを喜ばせるために魔法の果実を持って行きました

and she set out, trusting in the lamp
そして、ランプを信じて出発しました
The Grand Vizier and the lords of council had just gone into the palace
大宰相と評議会の諸侯は宮殿に入ったところだった
and she placed herself in front of the Sultan
そして彼女はスルタンの前に身を置いた
He, however, took no notice of her
しかし、彼は彼女に気づかなかった
She went every day for a week
彼女は一週間毎日通った
and she stood in the same place
そして彼女は同じ場所に立っていた
When the council broke up on the sixth day the Sultan said to his Vizier:
6日目に評議会が解散したとき、スルタンは宰相に言った
"I see a certain woman in the audience-chamber every day"
「私は毎日、謁見の間にいるある女性を見かけます」
"she is always carrying something in a napkin"
彼女はいつもナプキンに何かを入れて持ち歩いている
"Call her to come to us, next time"
今度、彼女を呼んで、私たちのところに来てください
"so that I may find out what she wants"
「彼女が何を望んでいるのかを知るために」
Next day the Vizier gave her a sign
翌日、宰相は彼女に合図をした
she went up to the foot of the throne
彼女は玉座のふもとに上がった
and she remained kneeling till the Sultan spoke to her
そして、スルタンが彼女に話しかけるまで、彼女はひざまずいたままでした
"Rise, good woman, tell me what you want"
「立ち上がれ、いい女よ、何が欲しいのか教えて」

She hesitated, so the Sultan sent away all but the Vizier
彼女は躊躇したので、スルタンは宰相以外全員を送り出した
and he bade her to speak frankly
そして、彼は彼女に率直に話すように命じました
and he promised to forgive her for anything she might say
そして、彼女が何を言おうと、彼は彼女を許すと約束しました
She then told him of her son's violent love for the Princess
そして、息子の王女への激しい愛を彼に話しました
"I prayed him to forget her" she said
「私は彼に彼女のことを忘れるように祈りました」と彼女は言った
"but the prayers were in vain"
「しかし、祈りは無駄だった」
"he threatened to do some desperate deed if I refused to go"
「私が行くのを拒んだら、必死のことをすると脅した」
"and so I ask your Majesty for the hand of the Princess"
「それで、陛下に姫様の手をお願いします」
"but now I pray you to forgive me"
「でも今は、どうかお許しください」
"and I pray that you forgive my son Aladdin"
「そして、息子のアラジンを許してくださるよう祈っています」
The Sultan asked her kindly what she had in the napkin
スルタンは優しく彼女にナプキンの中身を尋ねました
so she unfolded the napkin
そこで彼女はナプキンを広げた
and she presented the jewels to the Sultan
そして彼女は宝石をスルタンに贈りました
He was thunderstruck by the beauty of the jewels

彼は宝石の美しさに雷に打たれました
and he turned to the Vizier and asked "What sayest thou?"
そして宰相の方を向いて、「あなたは何とおっしゃいますか」と尋ねました。
"Ought I not to bestow the Princess on one who values her at such a price?"
「そんな値段で姫様を高く評価する者に、姫様を授けるべきではないでしょうか?」
The Vizier wanted her for his own son
宰相は彼女を自分の息子に欲しがった
so he begged the Sultan to withhold her for three months
そこで彼はスルタンに3ヶ月間彼女を差し控えるよう懇願した
perhaps within the time his son would contrive to make a richer present
もしかしたら、息子がもっと豊かなプレゼントを作ろうと画策するかもしれない
The Sultan granted the wish of his Vizier
スルタンは宰相の願いを叶えた
and he told Aladdin's mother that he consented to the marriage
そして、彼はアラジンの母親に結婚に同意したと言いました
but she must not appear before him again for three months
しかし、彼女は3ヶ月間、再び彼の前に現れてはならない

Aladdin waited patiently for nearly three months
アラジンは3ヶ月近く辛抱強く待っていました
after two months had elapsed his mother went to go to the market
2ヶ月が過ぎた頃、母親は市場に行きました

she was going into the city to buy oil
彼女は石油を買うために街に行っていた
when she got to the market found every one rejoicing
市場に着くと、みんなが喜んでいました
so she asked what was going on
そこで彼女は、何が起こっているのか尋ねました
"Do you not know?" was the answer
「知らないの?」というのが答えでした
"the son of the Grand Vizier is to marry the Sultan's daughter tonight"
「大宰相の息子は今夜、スルタンの娘と結婚することになっている」
Breathless, she ran and told Aladdin
息を切らしながら、彼女は走ってアラジンに言った
at first Aladdin was overwhelmed
最初、アラジンは圧倒されました
but then he thought of the lamp and rubbed it
しかし、ランプのことを思い出し、こすってみました
once again the the genie appeared out of the lamp
再び精霊がランプから現れた
"What is thy will?" asked the genie
「おまえの意志は?」と魔神は尋ねた
"The Sultan, as thou knowest, has broken his promise to me"
「スルタンは、汝の知る通り、私との約束を破った」
"the Vizier's son is to have the Princess"
「宰相の息子は王女を娶る」
"My command is that tonight you bring the bride and bridegroom"
「今夜、花嫁と花婿を連れてきなさい」
"Master, I obey" said the genie
「ご主人様、私は従います」と魔神は言いました
Aladdin then went to his chamber
その後、アラジンは自分の部屋に行きました

sure enough, at midnight the genie transported a bed
案の定、真夜中に魔神はベッドを運んでくれた
and the bed contained the Vizier's son and the Princess
ベッドには宰相の息子と王女がいました
"Take this new-married man, genie" he said
「この新婚の男を連れて行け、魔神」と彼は言った
"put him outside in the cold for the night"
「寒い中、一晩外に置いておけ」
"then return them again at daybreak"
「じゃあ、夜明けにまた返して」
So the genie took the Vizier's son out of bed
そこで魔神は宰相の息子をベッドから連れ出しました
and he left Aladdin with the Princess
そして彼はアラジンをプリンセスに預けました
"Fear nothing," Aladdin said to her, "you are my wife"
「何も恐れることはない」とアラジンは彼女に言った、「あなたは私の妻です」
"you were promised to me by your unjust father"
「お前は不当な父から約束された」
"and no harm shall come to you"
「そうすれば、あなたに危害が及ぶことはない」
The Princess was too frightened to speak
お姫様は怖くて何も言えませんでした
and she passed the most miserable night of her life
そして、彼女は人生で最も惨めな夜を過ごしました
although Aladdin lay down beside her and slept soundly
アラジンは彼女のそばに横になり、ぐっすり眠っていましたが
At the appointed hour the genie fetched in the shivering bridegroom
約束の時間に、精霊は震えている花婿を連れて来ました
he laid him in his place
彼は彼を彼の場所に横たえました

and he transported the bed back to the palace
そして、ベッドを宮殿に運びました
Presently the Sultan came to wish his daughter good-morning
やがてスルタンは娘におはようを言いに来た
The unhappy Vizier's son jumped up and hid himself
不幸な宰相の息子は飛び起きて身を隠しました
and the Princess would not say a word
お姫様は一言も言いません
and she was very sorrowful
そして、彼女はとても悲しんでいました
The Sultan sent her mother to her
スルタンは彼女の母親を彼女に送りました
"Why will you not speak to your father, child?"
「子よ、なぜ父に話さないのか」
"What has happened?" she asked
「どうしたの?」彼女は尋ねた
The Princess sighed deeply
王女は深いため息をついた
and at last she told her mother what had happened
そしてとうとう、何が起こったのかを母親に話しました
she told her how the bed had been carried into some strange house
彼女は、ベッドが見知らぬ家に運ばれてきた経緯を話した
and she told of what had happened in the house
そして、その家で起こったことを話しました
Her mother did not believe her in the least
彼女の母親は彼女を少しも信じませんでした
and she bade her to consider it an idle dream
そして、彼女はそれを怠惰な夢だとみなすようにと彼女に命じた
The following night exactly the same thing happened
次の夜も、まったく同じことが起こりました

and the next morning the princess wouldn't speak either
そして翌朝、お姫様も話さなくなりました
on the Princess's refusal to speak, the Sultan threatened to cut off her head
王女が話すことを拒むと、スルタンは王女の首を切り落とすと脅した
She then confessed all that had happened
その後、彼女は起こったことをすべて告白しました
and she bid him to ask the Vizier's son
そして、宰相の息子に尋ねるように命じました
The Sultan told the Vizier to ask his son
スルタンは宰相に息子に尋ねるように言いました
and the Vizier's son told the truth
そして宰相の息子は真実を語った
he added that he dearly loved the Princess
彼は王女を心から愛していると付け加えた
"but I would rather die than go through another such fearful night"
「でも、あんな恐ろしい夜をまた経験するくらいなら、死んだ方がましだ」
and he wished to be separated from her, which was granted
そして、彼は彼女から離れることを望み、それは叶えられました
and there was an end to feasting and rejoicing
そして、祝宴と歓喜には終わりがあった

then the three months were over
そして、3ヶ月が終わりました
Aladdin sent his mother to remind the Sultan of his promise
アラジンはスルタンに約束を思い出させるために母親を送りました
She stood in the same place as before

彼女は以前と同じ場所に立っていた
the Sultan had forgotten Aladdin
スルタンはアラジンを忘れていた
but at once he remembered him again
しかし、すぐに彼は再び彼のことを思い出しました
and he asked for her to come to him
そして、彼は彼女に自分のところに来るように頼みました
On seeing her poverty the Sultan felt less inclined than ever to keep his word
彼女の貧しさを見て、スルタンはかつてないほど約束を守る気になれなくなった
and he asked his Vizier's advice
そして彼は宰相に助言を求めた
he counselled him to set a high value on the Princess
彼は王女に高い価値を置くように彼に助言しました
a price so high that no man living could come up to it
生きている人間がそれに立ち向かうことができないほどの高値
The Sultan then turned to Aladdin's mother, saying:
スルタンはアラジンの母親に向かってこう言いました。
"Good woman, a Sultan must remember his promises"
「いい女よ、スルタンは約束を守らねばならない」
"and I will remember my promise"
「約束を忘れない」
"but your son must first send me forty basins of gold"
「しかし、あなたの息子は、まず金の入った40の盆を私に送らなければなりません。」
"and the gold basins must be brimful of jewels"
「そして、金の盆地は宝石であふれているに違いない」
"and they must be carried by forty black camels"
「四十頭の黒らくだに乗せられなければならない」
"and in front of each black camel there is to be a white one"

「そして、それぞれの黒いラクダの前には、白いラクダがいる」
"and they are all to be splendidly dressed"
「そして、彼らは皆、立派な服を着なければならない」
"Tell him that I await his answer"
「私が彼の答えを待っていると彼に伝えてください」
The mother of Aladdin bowed low
アラジンの母親は低くお辞儀をした
and then she went home
そして彼女は家に帰った
although she thought all was lost
全てが失われたと思ったが
She gave Aladdin the message
彼女はアラジンにメッセージを伝えた
and she added, "He may wait long enough for your answer!"
そして、「彼はあなたの答えを十分長く待つかもしれません!」と付け加えました。
"Not so long as you think, mother" her son replied
「お母さん、あんたが思っている限りはね」と息子は答えた
"I would do a great deal more than that for the Princess"
「お姫様のためなら、それ以上のことをしてあげるわ」
and he summoned the genie again
そして彼は再び魔神を召喚した
and in a few moments the eighty camels arrived
しばらくすると、80頭のラクダが到着しました
and they took up all space in the small house and garden
そして、彼らは小さな家と庭のすべてのスペースを占領しました
Aladdin made them set out to the palace
アラジンは彼らを宮殿に向かわせた
and they were followed by his mother

そして、彼らの後には母親が続いた
They were very richly dressed
彼らはとても豪華な服を着ていました
and splendid jewels were on their girdles
そして、その帯には立派な宝石がついていました
and everyone crowded around to see them
そして、みんなが彼らを見ようと群がりました
and the basins of gold they carried on their backs
そして、彼らが背負った金の入った盆
They entered the palace of the Sultan
彼らはスルタンの宮殿に入った
and they kneeled before him in a semi circle
そして、かれらは、半円を描いてイエスの前にひざまずいた
and Aladdin's mother presented them to the Sultan
そしてアラジンの母親はそれらをスルタンに贈りました
He hesitated no longer, but said:
彼はもう躊躇せず、言った。
"Good woman, return to your son"
「いい女よ、息子のところに帰れ」
"tell him that I wait for him with open arms"
「両手を広げて彼を待っていると伝えてください」
She lost no time in telling Aladdin
彼女はアラジンに話すのに時間を無駄にしなかった
and she bid him make haste
そして彼女は彼に急ぐように命じた
But Aladdin first called for the genie
しかし、アラジンは最初に精霊を呼びました
"I want a scented bath" he said
「香りのよいお風呂が欲しい」と彼は言った
"and I want a horse more beautiful than the Sultan's"
「スルタンの馬よりも美しい馬が欲しい」
"and I want twenty servants to attend me"
「そして、20人の召使いに付き添ってもらいたい」

"and I also want six beautifully dressed servants to wait on my mother
「それに、美しく着飾った召使いを6人も入れて、お母さんを待っていてもらいたいのです
"and lastly, I want ten thousand pieces of gold in ten purses"
「そして最後に、10個の財布に1万枚の金貨が欲しい」
No sooner had he said what he wanted and it was done
彼が言いたいことを言うとすぐに、それは行われました
Aladdin mounted his beautiful horse
アラジンは彼の美しい馬に乗った
and he passed through the streets
そして彼は通りを通り抜けた
the servants cast gold into the crowd as they went
しもべたちは、行く先々で群衆に金を投げ入れました
Those who had played with him in his childhood knew him not
幼少期に彼と遊んだことのある人たちは、彼を知らなかった
he had grown very handsome
彼はとてもハンサムになっていました
When the Sultan saw him he came down from his throne
スルタンは彼を見ると、玉座から降りてきました
he embraced his new son in law with open arms
彼は両手を広げて義理の息子を抱きしめました
and he led him into a hall where a feast was spread
そして、ごちそうが広げられている広間に案内しました
he intended to marry him to the Princess that very day
彼はその日のうちに王女と結婚するつもりでした
But Aladdin refused to marry straight away
しかし、アラジンはすぐに結婚を拒否しました
"first I must build a palace fit for the princess"

「まず、お姫様にふさわしい宮殿を建てなければなりません」
and then he took his leave
そして、彼は休暇を取りました
Once home, he said to the genie:
家に帰ると、彼は精霊に言いました。
"Build me a palace of the finest marble"
「最高級の大理石の宮殿を建ててください」
"set the palace with jasper, agate, and other precious stones"
「碧玉、瑪瑙、その他の宝石で宮殿をセットする」
"In the middle you shall build me a large hall with a dome"
「真ん中に、ドームのある大きな広間を建ててください」
"its four walls will be of masses of gold and silver"
「その四つの城壁は金銀の塊である」
"and each wall will have six windows"
「そして、それぞれの壁には6つの窓があります」
"and the lattices of the windows will be set with precious jewels"
「そして、窓の格子には貴重な宝石がはめ込まれる」
"but there must be one window that is not decorated"
「しかし、装飾されていない窓が1つあるに違いない」
"go see that it gets done!"
「それが成し遂げられるのを見に行こう!」
The palace was finished by the next day
宮殿は翌日までに完成しました
the genie carried him to the new palace
魔神は彼を新しい宮殿に連れて行った
and he showed him how all his orders had been faithfully carried out
そして、すべての命令がいかに忠実に実行されたかを彼に示しました

even a velvet carpet had been laid from Aladdin's palace to the Sultan's
アラジンの宮殿からスルタンの宮殿までベルベットの絨毯が敷かれていました
Aladdin's mother then dressed herself carefully
その後、アラジンの母親は慎重に服を着ました
and she walked to the palace with her servants
そして、しもべたちと一緒に宮殿に歩いて行きました
and Aladdin followed her on horseback
そしてアラジンは馬に乗って彼女を追いかけました
The Sultan sent musicians with trumpets and cymbals to meet them
スルタンはトランペットとシンバルを持った音楽家を彼らに会うために送りました
so the air resounded with music and cheers
そのため、空気は音楽と歓声で響き渡りました
She was taken to the Princess, who saluted her
彼女は王女のところに連れて行かれ、王女は彼女に敬礼した
and she treated her with great honour
そして、彼女は彼女を非常に尊敬して扱いました
At night the Princess said good-by to her father
夜、お姫様はお父さんに別れを告げました
and she set out on the carpet for Aladdin's palace
そして、絨毯の上をアラジンの宮殿に向かいました
his mother was at her side
彼の母親は彼女のそばにいた
and they were followed by their entourage of servants
そして、召使の側近が続いた
She was charmed at the sight of Aladdin
彼女はアラジンの姿に魅了されました
and Aladdin ran to receive her into the palace
そしてアラジンは彼女を宮殿に迎えに走った
"Princess," he said "blame your beauty for my boldness

「お姫様、私の大胆さをあなたの美しさのせいにしてください」と彼は言いました
"I hope I have not displeased you"
「不愉快にさせなかったことを願っています」
she said she willingly obeyed her father in this matter
彼女はこの件に関して、喜んで父親に従ったと言いました
because she had seen that he is handsome
彼女は彼がハンサムであるのを見ていたので
After the wedding had taken place Aladdin led her into the hall
結婚式が行われた後、アラジンは彼女をホールに連れて行きました
here a feast was spread out in the hall
ここでは、広間にご馳走が広がっていました
and she supped with him
そして、彼女は彼と一緒に飲んだ
after eating they danced till midnight
食べた後、彼らは真夜中まで踊りました

The next day Aladdin invited the Sultan to see the palace
翌日、アラジンはスルタンを宮殿に招待しました
they entered the hall with the four-and-twenty windows
二人は四十二の窓のある広間に入った
the windows were decorated with rubies, diamonds, and emeralds
窓はルビー、ダイヤモンド、エメラルドで飾られていました
he cried "It is a world's wonder!"
彼は叫びました「それは世界の驚異です!」
"There is only one thing that surprises me"
「驚いたことが1つだけ」

"Was it by accident that one window was left unfinished?"
「窓が1つ残っていたのは偶然だったのか?」
"No, sir, it was done so by design" replied Aladdin
「いや、あれは意図的にそうなったんだ」とアラジンは答えた
"I wished your Majesty to have the glory of finishing this palace"
「陛下には、この宮殿を完成させる栄光を願っていました」
The Sultan was pleased to be given this honour
スルタンはこの栄誉を与えられたことを喜んでいました
and he sent for the best jewellers in the city
そして、彼は街で最高の宝石商を送りました
He showed them the unfinished window
彼は未完成の窓を彼らに見せた
and he bade them to decorate it like the others
そして、他の者たちと同じように飾るようにと命じました
"Sir" replied their spokesman
「サー」と彼らのスポークスマンは答えた
"we cannot find enough jewels"
「宝石が足りない」
so the Sultan had his own jewels fetched
それでスルタンは自分の宝石を取ってきてもらいました
but those jewels were soon soon used up too
しかし、それらの宝石もすぐに使い果たされました
even after a month's time the work was not half done
1ヶ月経っても、作業は半分も終わっていませんでした
Aladdin knew that their task was impossible
アラジンは、自分たちの仕事が不可能であることを知っていました
he bade them to undo their work
イエスは彼らに、その仕事を取り消すように命じた

and he bade them carry the jewels back
そして、宝石を運び返すように命じました
the genie finished the window at his command
魔神は彼の命令で窓を完成させた
The Sultan was surprised to receive his jewels again
スルタンは再び宝石を受け取ったことに驚きました
he visited Aladdin, who showed him the window finished
彼はアラジンを訪ね、アラジンは完成した窓を見せた
and the Sultan embraced his son in law
そしてスルタンは義理の息子を抱きしめた
meanwhile, the envious Vizier suspected the work of enchantment
一方、嫉妬深い宰相は魔法の仕業を疑っていた
Aladdin had won the hearts of the people by his gentle bearing
アラジンは、その優しい立ち居振る舞いで人々の心をつかんでいました
He was made captain of the Sultan's armies
彼はスルタンの軍隊の隊長になりました
and he won several battles for his army
そして、彼は彼の軍隊のためにいくつかの戦いに勝ちました
but he remained as modest and courteous as before
しかし、彼は以前と変わらず謙虚で礼儀正しいままでした
in this way he lived in peace and content for several years
このようにして、彼は数年間平和で満足して暮らしました
But far away in Africa the magician remembered Aladdin
しかし、遠く離れたアフリカの魔術師はアラジンを思い出しました

and by his magic arts he discovered Aladdin hadn't perished in the cave
そして、彼の魔法の芸術によって、彼はアラジンが洞窟で死んでいないことを発見しました
but instead of perishing he had escaped and married the princess
しかし、彼は死ぬのではなく、逃げ出し、王女と結婚しました
and now he was living in great honour and wealth
そして今、彼は大きな名誉と富の中で暮らしていました
He knew that the poor tailor's son could only have accomplished this by means of the lamp
彼は、貧しい仕立て屋の息子がランプを使ってしかこれを成し遂げられないことを知っていました
and he travelled night and day until he reached the city
そして、町に着くまで夜も昼も旅をしました
he was bent on making sure of Aladdin's ruin
彼はアラジンの破滅を確かめることに熱心だった
As he passed through the town he heard people talking
町を通り過ぎると、人々が話しているのが聞こえました
all they could talk about was a marvellous palace
彼らが話せるのは、素晴らしい宮殿のことだけだった
"Forgive my ignorance," he asked
「私の無知をお許しください」と彼は尋ねた
"what is this palace you speak of?"
「お前が言うこの宮殿って何だ?」
"Have you not heard of Prince Aladdin's palace?" was the reply
「アラジン王子の宮殿のことを聞いたことがないの?」というのが返事でした
"it is the greatest wonder of the world"
「それは世界の最大の驚異です」
"I will direct you to the palace, if you would like to see it"

「もしよろしければ、宮殿に案内します」
The magician thanked him for bringing him to the palace
魔術師は、自分を宮殿に連れてきてくれたことに感謝した

and having seen the palace, he knew that it had been raised by the Genie of the Lamp
そして、宮殿を見て、ランプの魔神によって建てられたことを知った

this made him half mad with rage
これは彼を怒りで半ば狂わせた

He determined to get hold of the lamp
彼はランプを手に入れようと決心しました

and he would again plunge Aladdin into the deepest poverty
そして、彼は再びアラジンを最も深い貧困に陥れるでしょう

Unluckily, Aladdin had gone a-hunting for eight days
不運なことに、アラジンは8日間狩りに出かけていました

this gave the magician plenty of time
これにより、マジシャンは十分な時間を得ることができました

He bought a dozen copper lamps
彼は1ダースの銅ランプを買った

and he put them into a basket
そして、それらを籠に入れた

and he went to the palace
そして宮殿に行った

"New lamps for old!" he exclaimed
「古いランプに新しいランプを!」と彼は叫んだ

and he was followed by a jeering crowd
そして、嘲笑する群衆が彼に続いた

The Princess was sitting in the hall of four-and-twenty windows

お姫様は四十二十窓の広間に座っていました
she sent a servant to find out what the noise was about
彼女は召使いを遣わして、その音が何であるかを調べました
the servant came back laughing so much that the Princess scolded her
召使いが大笑いして帰ってきたので、お姫様はお姫様を叱りました
"Madam," replied the servant
「奥様」と召使いは答えました
"who can help but laughing when you see such a thing?"
「あんなものを見て笑わずにはいられない」
"an old fool is offering to exchange fine new lamps for old ones"
「年老いた愚か者が、立派な新しいランプを古いランプと交換することを申し出ている」
Another servant, hearing this, spoke up
これを聞いたもう一人の召使いが声を上げた
"There is an old lamp on the cornice there which he can have"
「そこのコーニスには古いランプがあり、それを持つことができます」
this, of course, was the magic lamp
これはもちろん、魔法のランプでした
Aladdin had left it there, as he could not take it out hunting with him
アラジンは狩りに連れ出すことができなかったので、そこに置いたままにしていました
The Princess didn't know know the lamp's value
お姫様はランプの価値を知りませんでした
laughingly she bade the servant to exchange it
笑いながら、娘は召使いにそれを交換するように命じました

the servant took the lamp to the magician
召使いはランプを魔術師のところに持って行きました
"Give me a new lamp for this" she said
「これのために新しいランプをください」と彼女は言いました
He snatched it and bade the servant to take her choice
彼はそれをひったくり、召使いに彼女の選択を取るように命じました
and all the crowd jeered at the sight
そして、群衆は皆、その光景を嘲笑った
but the magician cared little for the crowd
しかし、魔術師は群衆をほとんど気にかけなかった
he left the crowd with the lamp he had set out to get
彼は、手に入れようとしたランプを持って群衆を去った
and he went out of the city gates to a lonely place
そして、町の門を出て、寂しいところへ行きました
there he remained till nightfall
かれは、日暮れまでそこに留まった
and it nightfall he pulled out the lamp and rubbed it
そして日が暮れると、ランプを取り出してこすった
The genie appeared to the magician
魔術師の前に現れた魔神は
and the magician made his command to the genie
そして魔術師は魔神に命令を下した
"carry me, the princess, and the palace to a lonely place in Africa"
「私と王女と宮殿をアフリカの寂しい場所に運んで」

Next morning the Sultan looked out of the window toward Aladdin's palace
翌朝、スルタンは窓からアラジンの宮殿の方を見た
and he rubbed his eyes when he saw the palace was gone
そして、宮殿がなくなったのを見て目をこすりました

He sent for the Vizier and asked what had become of the palace
彼は宰相を呼び寄せ、宮殿がどうなったのかと尋ねた
The Vizier looked out too, and was lost in astonishment
宰相も外を眺め、驚いて途方に暮れました
He again put it down to enchantment
彼は再びそれをエンチャントに落とした
and this time the Sultan believed him
そしてこの時、スルタンは彼を信じた
he sent thirty men on horseback to fetch Aladdin in chains
彼はアラジンを鎖につなぐために馬に乗った30人の男を送りました
They met him riding home
彼らは彼が家に帰るのを待っているのに会いました
they bound him and forced him to go with them on foot
彼らはイエスを縛り、徒歩で一緒に行くことを強要した
The people, however, who loved him, followed them to the palace
しかし、彼を愛する人々は、彼らを追って宮殿に向かいました
they would make sure that he came to no harm
彼らは、彼が危害を加えないようにするだろう
He was carried before the Sultan
彼はスルタンの前に運ばれました
and the Sultan ordered the executioner to cut off his head
スルタンは死刑執行人に命じて首を切り落とすよう命じた
The executioner made Aladdin kneel down before a block of wood
死刑執行人はアラジンを木の塊の前にひざまずかせた
he bandaged his eyes so that he could not see
彼は目に包帯を巻いて見えないようにした

and he raised his scimitar to strike
そして彼はシミターを振り上げて攻撃した
At that instant the Vizier saw the crowd had forced their way into the courtyard
その瞬間、宰相は群衆が中庭に押し入ったのを見た
they were scaling the walls to rescue Aladdin
彼らはアラジンを救うために壁をよじ登っていました
so he called to the executioner to halt
それで彼は死刑執行人に止めるように呼びかけました
The people, indeed, looked so threatening that the Sultan gave way
実際、人々はスルタンが道を譲るほど威嚇しているように見えた
and he ordered Aladdin to be unbound
そして彼はアラジンに縛りを解くように命じた
he pardoned him in the sight of the crowd
かれは、群衆の目の前で彼を赦した
Aladdin now begged to know what he had done
アラジンは自分が何をしたのか知りたいと懇願した
"False wretch!" said the Sultan "come thither"
「偽りの惨めなやつめ!」とスルタンは言いました。
he showed him from the window the place where his palace had stood
彼は窓から宮殿が建っていた場所を見せました
Aladdin was so amazed that he could not say a word
アラジンは驚きのあまり、何も言えませんでした
"Where is my palace and my daughter?" demanded the Sultan
「私の宮殿と娘はどこだ?」とスルタンは尋ねました
"For the first I am not so deeply concerned"
「初めて、私はそれほど深く心配していません」
"but my daughter I must have"
「しかし、私の娘は私が持っている必要があります」
"and you must find her or lose your head"

「そして、あなたは彼女を見つけなければなりません、さもなければあなたの頭を失わなければなりません」
Aladdin begged to be granted forty days in which to find her
アラジンは、彼女を見つけるために40日間を与えてほしいと懇願しました
he promised that if he failed he would return
失敗したら戻ってくると約束した
and on his return he would suffer death at the Sultan's pleasure
そして、帰国後、彼はスルタンの喜びで死ぬだろう
His prayer was granted by the Sultan
彼の祈りはスルタンによって叶えられました
and he went forth sadly from the Sultan's presence
そして、悲しそうにスルタンの前から出て行きました
For three days he wandered about like a madman
三日間、彼は狂人のようにさまよった
he asked everyone what had become of his palace
彼は自分の宮殿がどうなったのかと皆に尋ねました
but they only laughed and pitied him
しかし、彼らはただ笑い、彼を哀れむだけだった
He came to the banks of a river
彼は川のほとりに来ました
he knelt down to say his prayers before throwing himself in
彼はひざまずいて祈りを捧げた後、身を投げ出した
In so doing he rubbed the magic ring he still wore
そうして、彼はまだ身に着けている魔法の指輪をこすった
The genie he had seen in the cave appeared
洞窟で見た魔神が現れた
and he asked him what his will was
そして、彼は自分の意志が何であるかを尋ねました
"Save my life, genie" said Aladdin

「私の命を救ってください、精霊」とアラジンは言いました
"bring my palace back"
「私の宮殿を取り戻して」
"That is not in my power" said the genie
「それは私の力では無理だ」と魔神は言った
"I am only the Slave of the Ring"
「私は指輪の奴隷に過ぎない」
"you must ask him for the lamp"
「ランプを頼まなければならない」
"that might be true" said Aladdin
「そうかも知れない」とアラジンは言った
"but thou canst take me to the palace"
「しかし、あなたは私を宮殿に連れて行くことができます」
"set me down under my dear wife's window"
「愛する妻の窓の下に私を置いて」
He at once found himself in Africa
彼はすぐにアフリカにいることに気づきました
he was under the window of the Princess
彼は王女の窓の下にいました
and he fell asleep out of sheer weariness
そして、彼は全くの疲れから眠りに落ちた
He was awakened by the singing of the birds
彼は鳥のさえずりで目覚めました
and his heart was lighter than it was before
そして、彼の心は以前よりも軽くなった
He saw plainly that all his misfortunes were owing to the loss of the lamp
彼は、自分の不幸はすべてランプを失ったことによるものだとはっきりと見ました
and he vainly wondered who had robbed him of it
そして、誰がそれを奪ったのか、むなしく思いました

That morning the Princess rose earlier than she normally
その朝、お姫様はいつもより早く起きました
once a day she was forced to endure the magicians company
一日に一度、彼女はマジシャンズ・カンパニーに耐えることを余儀なくされた
She, however, treated him very harshly
しかし、彼女は彼を非常に厳しく扱いました
so he dared not live with her in the palace
それで、彼はあえて宮殿で彼女と一緒に暮らさなかった
As she was dressing, one of her women looked out and saw Aladdin
彼女が服を着ていると、女性の一人が外を見ると、アラジンが見えました
The Princess ran and opened the window
お姫様は走って窓を開けました
at the noise she made Aladdin looked up
彼女が発した物音に、アラジンは顔を上げた
She called to him to come to her
彼女は彼に自分のところに来るように呼びかけました
it was a great joy for the lovers to see each other again
恋人たちにとって、再会は大きな喜びでした
After he had kissed her Aladdin said:
彼が彼女にキスをした後、アラジンは言った:
"I beg of you, Princess, in God's name"
「王女、神の名においてお願いします」
"before we speak of anything else"
「他のことを話す前に」
"for your own sake and mine"
「あなた自身のために、そして私のために」
"tell me what has become of the old lamp"
「古いランプがどうなったか教えてください」

"I left it on the cornice in the hall of four-and-twenty windows"
「四十窓の廊下のコーニスの上に置いてきた」
"Alas!" she said, "I am the innocent cause of our sorrows"
「ああ!」と彼女は言った、「私は私たちの悲しみの無実の原因です」
and she told him of the exchange of the lamp
そして、ランプの交換のことを彼に話しました
"Now I know" cried Aladdin
「わかった」とアラジンは叫びました
"we have to thank the magician for this!"
「マジシャンに感謝しなきゃ!」
"Where is the lamp?"
「ランプはどこ?」
"He carries it about with him" said the Princess
「あの子はあれを持ち歩いているのよ」とお姫様は言いました
"I know he carries the lamp with him"
「彼がランプを持ち歩いているのは知っている」
"because he pulled it out of his breast to show me"
「だって、胸から抜いて見せてくれたんだもん」
"and he wishes me to break my faith with you and marry him"
「そして、彼は私があなたとの信仰を壊して彼と結婚することを望んでいます。」
"and he said you were beheaded by my father's command"
「父の命令で首をはねられたと」
"He is for ever speaking ill of you"
「彼はいつもあなたの悪口を言っている」
"but I only reply by my tears"
「しかし、私は涙でしか答えません」
"If I persist, I doubt not"

「私が固執するなら、私は疑わない」
"but he will use violence"
「しかし、彼は暴力を振るうだろう」
Aladdin comforted his wife
アラジンは妻を慰めた
and he left her for a while
そして、彼はしばらく彼女から離れました
He changed clothes with the first person he met in the town
町で最初に出会った人と着替えた
and having bought a certain powder, he returned to the Princess
そして、ある粉を買って、お姫様のところに戻りました
the Princess let him in by a little side door
お姫様は小さな通用口から彼を中に入れました
"Put on your most beautiful dress" he said to her
「いちばん美しいドレスを着てください」と彼は彼女に言いました
"receive the magician with smiles today"
「今日は笑顔でマジシャンを迎えてください」
"lead him to believe that you have forgotten me"
「あなたが私を忘れたと彼に信じ込ませなさい」
"Invite him to sup with you"
「彼を一緒に飲みに誘う」
"and tell him you wish to taste the wine of his country"
「そして、彼の国のワインを味わいたいと彼に伝えてください」
"He will be gone for some time"
「彼はしばらくいなくなるだろう」
"while he is gone I will tell you what to do"
「彼がいない間に、私はあなたに何をすべきか教えてあげる」
She listened carefully to Aladdin
彼女はアラジンの話に注意深く耳を傾けた

and when he left she arrayed herself beautifully
そして、彼が去ったとき、彼女は美しく身を並べました
she hadn't dressed like this since she had left her city
こんな格好は街を出て以来初めてだった
She put on a girdle and head-dress of diamonds
彼女はダイヤモンドのガードルとヘッドドレスを身に着けました
she was more beautiful than ever
彼女はかつてないほど美しかった
and she received the magician with a smile
そして、彼女は笑顔で魔術師を迎えました
"I have made up my mind that Aladdin is dead"
「アラジンは死んだと決めた」
"my tears will not bring him back to me"
「私の涙は彼を私の元に戻さない」
"so I am resolved to mourn no more"
「だから、もう嘆かないと決心した」
"therefore I invite you to sup with me"
それゆえ、私はあなたを私と一緒に食事に招待します
"but I am tired of the wines we have"
「でも、今あるワインにはうんざりだ」
"I would like to taste the wines of Africa"
「アフリカのワインを味わってみたい」
The magician ran to his cellar
魔術師は地下室に走った
and the Princess put the powder Aladdin had given her in her cup
そして、お姫様はアラジンがくれた粉をカップに入れました
When he returned she asked him to drink her health
彼が戻ってくると、彼女は彼に自分の健康を飲むように頼みました
and she handed him her cup in exchange for his

そして、彼女は彼のものと引き換えに自分の杯を彼に手渡した
this was done as a sign to show she was reconciled to him
これは、彼女が彼と和解したことを示すしるしとして行われました
Before drinking the magician made her a speech
飲む前に、マジシャンは彼女にスピーチをしました
he wanted to praise her beauty
彼は彼女の美しさを褒め称えたかった
but the Princess cut him short
しかし、王女は彼を短く切り捨てました
"Let us drink first"
「まずは飲もう」
"and you shall say what you will afterwards"
そして、あなたは後であなたが望むことを言うでしょう
She set her cup to her lips and kept it there
彼女はカップを唇に当て、そこに置いたままにした
the magician drained his cup to the dregs
魔術師は杯をカスに流してしまった
and upon finishing his drink he fell back lifeless
そして、飲み終えると、息絶えて倒れました
The Princess then opened the door to Aladdin
その後、プリンセスはアラジンのドアを開けました
and she flung her arms round his neck
そして彼女は彼の首に腕を回した
but Aladdin asked her to leave him
しかし、アラジンは彼女に彼から離れるように頼みました
there was still more to be done
やるべきことはまだまだあった
He then went to the dead magician
それから彼は死んだ魔術師のところへ行きました
and he took the lamp out of his vest

そして、上着からランプを取り出しました
he bade the genie to carry the palace back
彼は精霊に宮殿を運び返すように命じた
the Princess in her chamber only felt two little shocks
部屋にいた王女は、小さな衝撃を2回感じただけでした
in little time she was at home again
しばらくすると、彼女は再び家に帰った
The Sultan was sitting on his balcony
スルタンはバルコニーに座っていた
he was mourning for his lost daughter
彼は亡くなった娘を悼んでいた
he looked up and had to rub his eyes again
彼は顔を上げ、再び目をこすらなければならなかった
the palace stood there as it had before
宮殿は以前と変わらずそこに立っていた
He hastened over to the palace to see his daughter
王子は娘に会うために宮殿に急ぎました
Aladdin received him in the hall of the palace
アラジンは宮殿のホールで彼を迎えました
and the princess was at his side
そして、お姫様は彼のそばにいました
Aladdin told him what had happened
アラジンは彼に何が起こったのかを話しました
and he showed him the dead body of the magician
そして魔術師の死体を見せた
so that the Sultan would believe him
スルタンが彼を信じるように
A ten days' feast was proclaimed
10日間の祝宴が宣言された
and it seemed as if Aladdin might now live the rest of his life in peace
そして、アラジンは今、残りの人生を平和に暮らすことができるように見えました
but it was not to be as peaceful as he had hoped

しかし、それは彼が望んでいたほど平和ではありませんでした

The African magician had a younger brother
アフリカの魔術師には弟がいた

he was maybe even more wicked and cunning than his brother
彼はおそらく兄よりも邪悪で狡猾だった

He travelled to Aladdin to avenge his brother's death
彼は兄の死の復讐のためにアラジンに旅しました

he went to visit a pious woman called Fatima
彼はファティマという敬虔な女性を訪ねました

he thought she might be of use to him
彼は彼女が自分にとって役に立つかもしれないと思った

He entered her cell and clapped a dagger to her breast
彼は彼女の独房に入り、彼女の胸に短剣を叩きつけた

then he told her to rise and do his bidding
それから彼は彼女に立ち上がって彼の命令に従うように言いました

and if she didn't he said he would kill her
そして、もし彼女がそうしなければ、彼は彼女を殺すと言いました

He changed his clothes with her
彼は彼女と服を着替えました

and he coloured his face like hers
そして、彼は彼女のように顔を染めました

he put on her veil so that he looked just like her
彼は彼女にそっくりになるように彼女のベールをかぶった

and finally he murdered her despite her compliance
そしてついに彼は、彼女が従ったにも関わらず、彼女を殺害した

so that she could tell no tales
歌詞の意味: 彼女は物語を話すことができないように

Then he went towards the palace of Aladdin
それから彼はアラジンの宮殿に向かいました
all the people thought he was the holy woman
人々は皆、イエスを聖なる女だと思った
they gathered round him to kiss his hands
彼らはイエスのまわりに集まって、イエスの手に接吻した
and they begged for his blessing
そして彼らはイエスの祝福を乞うた
When he got to the palace there a great commotion around him
王子が宮殿に着くと、周りは大騒ぎでした
the princess wanted to know what all the noise was about
お姫様は、この騒ぎが何なのか知りたがっていました
so she bade her servant to look out of the window for her
それで、娘は召使いに窓の外を見るように言いました
and her servant asked what the noise was all about
しもべは、その音は一体何なのかと尋ねました
she found out it was the holy woman causing the commotion
騒ぎを起こしたのは聖女だとわかった
she was curing people of their ailments by touching them
彼女は人々に触れることによって彼らの病気を治していました
the Princess had long desired to see Fatima
王女は長い間、ファティマに会いたいと願っていました
so she get her servant to ask her into the palace
それで、彼女は召使いに彼女を宮殿に呼ばせます
and the false Fatima accepted the offer into the palace
そして、偽のファーティマは宮殿への申し出を受け入れました

the magician offered up a prayer for her health and prosperity
魔術師は彼女の健康と繁栄を祈願した
the Princess made him sit by her
王女は彼を彼女のそばに座らせました
and she begged him to stay with her
そして、彼女は彼に一緒にいてほしいと懇願しました
The false Fatima wished for nothing better
偽りのファーティマは、それ以上のことは何も望まなかった
and she consented to the princess' wish
そして王女の願いを聞き入れました
but he kept his veil down
しかし、彼はベールを下ろしたままでした
because he knew that he would be discovered otherwise
そうでなければ発見されることを彼は知っていたからだ
The Princess showed him the hall
王女は彼に広間を見せました
and she asked him what he thought of it
そして、彼女は彼にそれについてどう思うか尋ねました
"It is truly beautiful" said the false Fatima
「ほんとうに美しいわ」と偽のファティマは言いました
"but in my mind your palace still wants one thing"
「しかし、私の心の中では、あなたの宮殿はまだ一つのことを望んでいます」
"And what is that?" asked the Princess
「それで、あれは何なの?」とお姫様は尋ねました
"If only a Roc's egg were hung up from the middle of this dome"
「このドームの真ん中からロックの卵が吊るされていたら」
"then it would be the wonder of the world" he said
「それなら、それは世界の驚異になるだろう」と彼は言った

After this the Princess could think of nothing but the Roc's egg
この後、王女はロックの卵のことしか考えられませんでした

when Aladdin returned from hunting he found her in a very ill humour
アラジンが狩りから戻ったとき、彼は彼女がとても不機嫌なのを見つけました

He begged to know what was amiss
彼は何がおかしいのか知りたいと懇願した

and she told him what had spoiled her pleasure
そして、彼女は自分の喜びを台無しにしたことを彼に話しました

"I'm made miserable for the want of a Roc's egg"
「ロックの卵が欲しくて惨めにされる」

"If that is all you want you shall soon be happy" replied Aladdin
「それだけなら、すぐに幸せになれるよ」とアラジンは答えました

he left her and rubbed the lamp
彼は彼女を残し、ランプをこすった

when the genie appeared he commanded him to bring a Roc's egg
魔神が現れたとき、彼はロックの卵を持ってくるように命じました

The genie gave such a loud and terrible shriek that the hall shook
魔神は大声で恐ろしい叫び声をあげたので、広間は揺れました

"Wretch!" he cried, "is it not enough that I have done everything for you?"
「惨めだ!」と彼は叫びました、「おれがおまえのために何でもしたのでは十分ではないのか?」

"but now you command me to bring my master"

「しかし、今、あなたは私に私の主人を連れて来るように命じます」
"and you want me to hang him up in the midst of this dome"
「そして、このドームの真ん中に吊るし上げて欲しい」
"You and your wife and your palace deserve to be burnt to ashes"
「お前とお前の妻とお前の宮殿は焼かれて灰になるに値する」
"but this request does not come from you"
「しかし、この要求はあなたから来たものではありません」
"the demand comes from the brother of the magician"
「魔術師の兄からの需要」
"the magician whom you have destroyed"
「お前が滅ぼした魔術師」
"He is now in your palace disguised as the holy woman"
「彼は今、聖女に変装してあなたの宮殿にいます」
"the real holy woman he has already murdered"
「彼がすでに殺した本物の聖女」
"it was him who put that wish into your wife's head"
「その願いを奥さんの頭に叩き込んだのは彼です」
"Take care of yourself, for he means to kill you"
「気をつけろ、お前を殺すつもりだから」
upon saying this the genie disappeared
そう言うと、魔神は姿を消した
Aladdin went back to the Princess
アラジンはプリンセスのところへ戻った
he told her that his head ached
彼は頭が痛いと彼女に言った
so she requested the holy Fatima to be fetched
そこで彼女は聖なるファーティマを連れて来るように頼みました
she could lay her hands on his head

彼女は彼の頭に両手を置くことができた
and his headache would be cured by her powers
そして彼の頭痛は彼女の力によって治されるだろう
when the magician came near Aladdin seized his dagger
魔術師が近づくと、アラジンは短剣をつかんだ
and he pierced him in the heart
そして彼は彼の心臓を突き刺した
"What have you done?" cried the Princess
「何をしたの?」とお姫様は叫びました
"You have killed the holy woman!"
「お前は聖女を殺した!」
"It is not so" replied Aladdin
「そうじゃない」とアラジンは答えました
"I have killed a wicked magician"
「私は邪悪な魔術師を殺した」
and he told her of how she had been deceived
そして、彼女がいかに騙されたかを彼女に話しました
After this Aladdin and his wife lived in peace
この後、アラジンと彼の妻は平和に暮らしました
He succeeded the Sultan when he died
スルタンが亡くなったとき、彼はスルタンの後を継いだ
he reigned over the kingdom for many years
彼は長年にわたって王国を治めました
and he left behind him a long lineage of kings
そして、彼は長い王の血統を残しました

The End
最後です

www.tranzlaty.com

www.ingramcontent.com/pod-product-compliance
Lightning Source LLC
Chambersburg PA
CBHW011954090526
44591CB00020B/2768